40 Cheese Recipes for Home

By: Kelly Johnson

Table of Contents

- Mushroom and Fontina Flatbread
- Prosciutto and Fig Pizza

Desserts:

- Cheesecake with Raspberry Coulis
- Chocolate Fondue with Assorted Dippers
- Ricotta and Honey Tart
- Blueberry Cheesecake Bars
- Cheddar Apple Pie

Breakfast:

- Cheese and Herb Omelette
- Cheese and Spinach Breakfast Casserole
- Cheese and Ham Quiche
- Cheese Danish
- Cheese and Tomato Breakfast Sandwich

Breads and Rolls:

- Garlic Parmesan Breadsticks
- Cheddar Jalapeños Cornbread
- Cheese and Herb Focaccia
- Swiss Cheese and Onion Bread
- Cheese-Stuffed Pretzels

Appetizers:

Cheese and Charcuterie Board

Ingredients:

Cheeses:

> Brie
> Camembert
> Gouda
> Blue Cheese
> Manchego
> Goat Cheese (Chevre)
> Cheddar
> Swiss
> Provolone

Charcuterie:

10. Prosciutto

> Salami (Genoa, Soppressata)
> Chorizo
> Mortadella
> Coppa
> Smoked Ham

Accompaniments:

16. Crackers (Variety of Types)

> Baguette Slices
> Grapes (Red and Green)
> Fig Jam
> Honey
> Dijon Mustard
> Olives (Variety of Types)
> Pickles (Cornichons)

Nuts (Almonds, Walnuts)
Dried Fruits (Apricots, Figs)

Extras:

26. Dark Chocolate

Cherry Tomatoes
Radishes
Pâté
Marinated Artichokes

Instructions:

Arrange Cheeses:
- Place a variety of cheeses on the board, spacing them out for easy access. Consider different textures and flavors.

Add Charcuterie:
- Arrange cured meats around the cheeses, creating a visually appealing display.

Arrange Accompaniments:
- Position crackers and baguette slices to fill gaps on the board. Add small bowls or jars for fig jam, honey, and Dijon mustard.

Incorporate Fruits and Nuts:
- Scatter grapes, dried fruits, and nuts around the board for a mix of sweet and savory bites.

Include Pickles and Olives:
- Place pickles, such as cornichons, and an assortment of olives in small clusters.

Add Extras for Variety:
- Intersperse extras like dark chocolate, cherry tomatoes, radishes, and marinated artichokes for additional flavors.

Create a Balanced Spread:
- Aim for a balanced distribution of flavors and textures across the board.

Serve at Room Temperature:
- Allow cheeses and charcuterie to come to room temperature before serving for optimal flavor.

Encourage Pairing:
- Provide a variety of pairings, such as pairing blue cheese with honey or prosciutto with fig jam.

Enjoy:

- Invite guests to enjoy the variety of flavors and textures by trying different combinations.

A well-crafted Cheese and Charcuterie Board is a versatile and elegant way to entertain. Customize the selection based on your preferences and availability, and feel free to experiment with different combinations to suit your taste. Enjoy the delightful experience of sharing and savoring the delicious offerings on the board!

Baked Brie with Honey and Nuts

Ingredients:

- 1 wheel of Brie cheese (8-ounce)
- 1/4 cup honey
- 1/4 cup chopped mixed nuts (such as walnuts, pecans, or almonds)
- Fresh rosemary sprigs (for garnish, optional)
- Baguette slices or crackers (for serving)

Instructions:

Preheat the Oven:
- Preheat your oven to 350°F (175°C).

Prepare the Brie:
- Remove any packaging from the Brie wheel. If desired, you can leave the rind on for baking, or you can score the top of the Brie lightly with a knife.

Place on Baking Dish:
- Place the Brie wheel in a small baking dish or on a parchment-lined baking sheet.

Drizzle with Honey:
- Drizzle the honey over the top of the Brie, ensuring it covers the surface evenly.

Sprinkle with Nuts:
- Sprinkle the chopped nuts over the honey-covered Brie, pressing them gently into the cheese.

Bake in the Oven:
- Bake the Brie in the preheated oven for approximately 10-15 minutes, or until the cheese is soft and gooey. Keep an eye on it to prevent over-baking.

Garnish (Optional):
- If desired, garnish the baked Brie with fresh rosemary sprigs for a fragrant and decorative touch.

Serve Warm:
- Remove the baked Brie from the oven and let it cool for a couple of minutes. Baked Brie is best served warm and gooey.

Serve with Baguette or Crackers:
- Arrange baguette slices or crackers around the baked Brie for dipping and spreading.

Enjoy:
- Dig in and enjoy the creamy, honey-infused goodness of the Baked Brie with a delightful crunch from the nuts!

This Baked Brie with Honey and Nuts is a simple yet elegant appetizer that's perfect for entertaining. The warm, gooey Brie pairs beautifully with the sweetness of honey and the nutty crunch of chopped nuts. Serve it with baguette slices or crackers, and watch it disappear as your guests savor the delicious combination of flavors and textures.

Caprese Skewers with Mozzarella

Ingredients:

- Fresh mozzarella balls (bocconcini)
- Cherry tomatoes
- Fresh basil leaves
- Balsamic glaze
- Extra virgin olive oil
- Salt and pepper, to taste
- Wooden skewers

Instructions:

Prepare Skewers:
- If using wooden skewers, soak them in water for about 30 minutes to prevent them from splintering. This step is especially important if you plan to grill the skewers.

Assemble Ingredients:
- Gather the fresh mozzarella balls, cherry tomatoes, and fresh basil leaves. Ensure that the mozzarella balls are drained if stored in water.

Thread Ingredients:
- Begin assembling the skewers by threading a cherry tomato onto the skewer, followed by a fresh basil leaf, and then a mozzarella ball. Repeat this pattern until the skewer is filled, leaving a little space at the ends for easy handling.

Arrange on a Platter:
- Arrange the Caprese skewers on a serving platter or dish.

Season with Salt and Pepper:
- Lightly sprinkle the skewers with salt and pepper to enhance the flavors.

Drizzle with Olive Oil:
- Drizzle extra virgin olive oil over the skewers for added richness.

Drizzle with Balsamic Glaze:
- Finish the Caprese skewers by drizzling balsamic glaze over them. This adds a sweet and tangy flavor to the dish.

Serve Immediately:
- Serve the Caprese skewers immediately for the freshest taste and best texture.

Enjoy:
- Enjoy this classic and refreshing appetizer as a light and flavorful addition to your gathering or as a simple snack!

Caprese Skewers with Mozzarella are a delightful and visually appealing appetizer. The combination of fresh mozzarella, cherry tomatoes, and basil creates a burst of flavor in every bite. Drizzling them with balsamic glaze and olive oil adds a touch of richness. These skewers are perfect for parties, picnics, or any occasion where you want to impress with a taste of Italy!

Cheese-Stuffed Mushrooms

Ingredients:

- 16-20 large white mushrooms, cleaned and stems removed
- 1 tablespoon olive oil
- 1 small onion, finely chopped
- 2 cloves garlic, minced
- 8 ounces cream cheese, softened
- 1/2 cup grated Parmesan cheese
- 1/2 cup shredded mozzarella cheese
- 1/4 cup breadcrumbs
- 2 tablespoons fresh parsley, chopped
- Salt and black pepper, to taste
- Cooking spray or melted butter (for greasing)

Instructions:

Preheat the Oven:
- Preheat your oven to 375°F (190°C).

Prepare the Mushrooms:
- Clean the mushrooms with a damp cloth to remove any dirt. Gently twist and remove the stems, creating a hollow space for the stuffing. Set aside.

Sauté Onion and Garlic:
- In a skillet, heat olive oil over medium heat. Sauté chopped onion until translucent, then add minced garlic and cook for an additional 1-2 minutes. Remove from heat and let it cool.

Prepare the Filling:
- In a mixing bowl, combine the cream cheese, grated Parmesan, shredded mozzarella, breadcrumbs, chopped parsley, sautéed onion, and garlic. Mix well until all ingredients are evenly incorporated. Season with salt and black pepper to taste.

Stuff the Mushrooms:
- Using a spoon or your hands, stuff each mushroom cap generously with the cheese mixture, mounding it slightly.

Arrange on a Baking Sheet:
- Place the stuffed mushrooms on a baking sheet, lightly greased with cooking spray or melted butter.

Bake in the Oven:

- Bake in the preheated oven for 20-25 minutes or until the mushrooms are tender and the cheese is golden brown and bubbly.

Serve Warm:
- Remove from the oven and let the cheese-stuffed mushrooms cool for a few minutes before serving.

Garnish (Optional):
- Garnish with additional chopped parsley if desired.

Enjoy:
- Serve these delicious cheese-stuffed mushrooms as an appetizer or a tasty party snack. They're best enjoyed warm!

These Cheese-Stuffed Mushrooms are a crowd-pleasing appetizer with a creamy and savory filling. The combination of cream cheese, Parmesan, and mozzarella creates a rich and gooey texture, while breadcrumbs add a subtle crunch. Whether you're entertaining guests or enjoying a cozy night in, these stuffed mushrooms are sure to be a hit!

Spinach and Artichoke Dip

Ingredients:

- 1 (10-ounce) package frozen chopped spinach, thawed and drained
- 1 (14-ounce) can artichoke hearts, drained and chopped
- 1 cup mayonnaise
- 1 cup sour cream
- 1 cup grated Parmesan cheese
- 1 cup shredded mozzarella cheese
- 1 teaspoon minced garlic
- 1/2 teaspoon onion powder
- 1/2 teaspoon dried oregano
- 1/2 teaspoon dried basil
- 1/4 teaspoon salt
- 1/4 teaspoon black pepper
- 1/4 teaspoon red pepper flakes (optional, for a hint of heat)
- Cooking spray or olive oil (for greasing)
- Baguette slices, tortilla chips, or vegetable sticks (for serving)

Instructions:

Preheat the Oven:
- Preheat your oven to 375°F (190°C).

Prepare Spinach and Artichokes:
- Thaw the frozen chopped spinach and squeeze out any excess water. Chop the artichoke hearts into smaller pieces.

Mix Ingredients:
- In a large mixing bowl, combine the drained spinach, chopped artichokes, mayonnaise, sour cream, grated Parmesan cheese, shredded mozzarella cheese, minced garlic, onion powder, dried oregano, dried basil, salt, black pepper, and red pepper flakes (if using). Mix until all ingredients are well combined.

Grease Baking Dish:
- Lightly grease a baking dish with cooking spray or a thin layer of olive oil.

Transfer Mixture to Baking Dish:
- Transfer the spinach and artichoke mixture to the prepared baking dish, spreading it evenly.

Bake in the Oven:
- Bake in the preheated oven for 25-30 minutes or until the dip is hot and bubbly, and the top is golden brown.

Broil (Optional):

- If desired, broil for an additional 1-2 minutes to achieve a golden, slightly crispy top.

Serve Warm:

- Remove from the oven and let it cool slightly before serving.

Serve with Dippers:

- Serve the Spinach and Artichoke Dip with baguette slices, tortilla chips, or vegetable sticks for dipping.

Enjoy:

- Enjoy this creamy and flavorful Spinach and Artichoke Dip as a crowd-pleasing appetizer for parties, gatherings, or a cozy night in!

This Spinach and Artichoke Dip is a classic and irresistible appetizer that combines the richness of cheese with the freshness of spinach and artichokes. Whether you're hosting a party or simply craving a delicious dip, this recipe is sure to be a hit. Serve it warm with your favorite dippers and watch it disappear!

Soups and Salads:

Broccoli Cheddar Soup

Ingredients:

- 1/4 cup unsalted butter
- 1 onion, finely chopped
- 2 cloves garlic, minced
- 1/4 cup all-purpose flour
- 4 cups fresh broccoli florets, chopped
- 4 cups low-sodium chicken or vegetable broth
- 2 cups whole milk
- 2 cups shredded sharp cheddar cheese
- Salt and black pepper, to taste
- 1/4 teaspoon nutmeg (optional, for added depth)
- Croutons or extra shredded cheddar for garnish (optional)

Instructions:

Sauté Onion and Garlic:
- In a large pot or Dutch oven, melt the butter over medium heat. Add the chopped onion and sauté until softened, about 3-4 minutes. Add minced garlic and sauté for an additional 1-2 minutes until fragrant.

Add Flour:
- Sprinkle the flour over the sautéed onions and garlic. Stir continuously to form a roux, cooking for 2-3 minutes to eliminate the raw flour taste.

Add Broccoli:
- Add the chopped broccoli florets to the pot. Stir to coat the broccoli with the roux.

Pour in Broth and Milk:
- Gradually pour in the chicken or vegetable broth and whole milk, stirring constantly to avoid lumps. Bring the mixture to a simmer.

Simmer Until Broccoli is Tender:
- Reduce heat to medium-low and simmer the soup uncovered until the broccoli is tender, about 15-20 minutes.

Blend Soup (Optional):
- For a smoother texture, use an immersion blender to blend the soup to your desired consistency. Alternatively, transfer a portion of the soup to a blender, blend, and return it to the pot.

Add Cheddar Cheese:

- Gradually add the shredded cheddar cheese to the soup, stirring until the cheese is melted and the soup is smooth.

Season with Spices:

- Season the soup with salt, black pepper, and nutmeg (if using). Adjust the seasoning according to your taste.

Serve:

- Ladle the Broccoli Cheddar Soup into bowls. Garnish with croutons or extra shredded cheddar if desired.

Enjoy:

- Serve this comforting Broccoli Cheddar Soup hot and enjoy the rich, cheesy goodness!

This homemade Broccoli Cheddar Soup is a classic comfort dish with a creamy and cheesy base complemented by tender broccoli florets. It's perfect for warming up on a chilly day or serving as a comforting meal. Customize the thickness and texture to your liking, and savor the delicious combination of flavors in every spoonful!

Caesar Salad with Parmesan Crisps

Ingredients:

For Caesar Salad:

- 1 large head of romaine lettuce, washed and chopped
- 1 cup croutons
- 1/2 cup freshly grated Parmesan cheese
- Caesar dressing (store-bought or homemade)

For Parmesan Crisps:

- 1 cup freshly grated Parmesan cheese

Instructions:

Prepare Parmesan Crisps:

Preheat the Oven:
- Preheat your oven to 375°F (190°C).

Line Baking Sheet:
- Line a baking sheet with parchment paper.

Create Crisps:
- Spoon small heaps (about 1 tablespoon each) of grated Parmesan cheese onto the prepared baking sheet, leaving space between each heap.

Flatten and Shape:
- Use the back of a spoon to gently flatten and shape each heap into a thin, round disc. Ensure they are evenly spaced.

Bake in the Oven:
- Bake in the preheated oven for 5-7 minutes or until the edges are golden brown and the cheese has melted and crisped up.

Cool:
- Allow the Parmesan crisps to cool completely on the baking sheet. They will continue to firm up as they cool.

Remove from Baking Sheet:
- Once cooled and firm, carefully peel the Parmesan crisps off the parchment paper.

Assemble Caesar Salad:

Prepare Romaine Lettuce:
- Wash and chop the romaine lettuce, then place it in a large salad bowl.

Add Croutons:
- Add croutons to the salad bowl, distributing them evenly.

Grate Parmesan:
- Grate additional Parmesan cheese over the salad for extra flavor.

Toss with Caesar Dressing:
- Drizzle Caesar dressing over the salad to your liking. Toss the salad gently to ensure even dressing distribution.

Garnish with Parmesan Crisps:
- Just before serving, garnish the Caesar Salad with the homemade Parmesan crisps for an extra crunchy and cheesy element.

Serve Immediately:
- Serve the Caesar Salad immediately, ensuring the Parmesan crisps stay crisp.

Enjoy:
- Enjoy this classic Caesar Salad with a delightful twist of homemade Parmesan crisps for added texture and flavor!

This Caesar Salad with Parmesan Crisps combines the freshness of romaine lettuce, the crunch of croutons, and the savory goodness of Parmesan crisps. The homemade Parmesan crisps add an extra layer of texture and a burst of cheesy flavor to elevate the classic Caesar Salad. Perfect as a refreshing side or a light meal on its own!

Caprese Salad with Fresh Mozzarella

Ingredients:

- 4 large ripe tomatoes, sliced
- 1 pound fresh mozzarella cheese, sliced
- Fresh basil leaves
- Extra virgin olive oil
- Balsamic glaze
- Salt and black pepper, to taste
- Optional: Freshly ground black pepper, chopped fresh basil for garnish

Instructions:

Prepare Tomatoes and Mozzarella:
- Wash and slice the tomatoes and fresh mozzarella cheese into uniform slices.

Assemble Salad:
- Arrange the tomato and mozzarella slices on a serving platter in an alternating pattern. Tuck fresh basil leaves between the tomato and mozzarella slices.

Drizzle Olive Oil:
- Drizzle extra virgin olive oil over the tomato and mozzarella slices. Ensure each slice is lightly coated.

Balsamic Glaze:
- Drizzle balsamic glaze over the salad for a sweet and tangy flavor. You can create a decorative pattern if desired.

Season with Salt and Pepper:
- Sprinkle salt and black pepper to taste over the salad. Adjust the seasoning according to your preference.

Garnish (Optional):
- Optionally, garnish the Caprese Salad with freshly ground black pepper and chopped fresh basil for an extra burst of flavor and color.

Serve Fresh:
- Serve the Caprese Salad immediately to enjoy the freshness of the ingredients.

Enjoy:
- Delight in the simple and vibrant flavors of this classic Caprese Salad with fresh mozzarella, tomatoes, and basil!

This Caprese Salad with Fresh Mozzarella is a timeless Italian dish that celebrates the simplicity of high-quality ingredients. The combination of ripe tomatoes, creamy fresh mozzarella, and fragrant basil drizzled with olive oil and balsamic glaze creates a refreshing and flavorful salad. Serve it as a light appetizer or a side dish to complement any meal.

Gruyere French Onion Soup

Ingredients:

- 4 large onions, thinly sliced
- 1/4 cup unsalted butter
- 2 cloves garlic, minced
- 1 teaspoon granulated sugar
- 1/2 cup dry white wine (optional)
- 4 cups beef broth
- 2 cups chicken broth
- 1/2 teaspoon dried thyme
- Salt and black pepper, to taste
- Baguette slices
- 2 cups Gruyère cheese, shredded

Instructions:

Caramelize Onions:
- In a large pot, melt butter over medium heat. Add thinly sliced onions and cook, stirring occasionally, until the onions are soft and deeply caramelized. This may take 30-40 minutes.

Add Garlic and Sugar:
- Add minced garlic to the caramelized onions and cook for an additional 1-2 minutes. Sprinkle sugar over the onions and continue cooking to enhance caramelization.

Deglaze with White Wine (Optional):
- Pour in the dry white wine to deglaze the pot, scraping up any browned bits from the bottom. Allow the wine to cook down for a few minutes.

Add Broths and Thyme:
- Pour in both beef and chicken broths, and add dried thyme. Season with salt and black pepper to taste. Bring the soup to a simmer and let it cook for an additional 15-20 minutes to meld the flavors.

Preheat Broiler:
- Preheat your broiler.

Prepare Baguette Slices:
- Toast baguette slices under the broiler until golden brown on both sides.

Ladle Soup into Oven-Safe Bowls:
- Ladle the French onion soup into oven-safe bowls, leaving some space at the top.

Top with Gruyère:
- Place a toasted baguette slice on top of each bowl of soup. Generously sprinkle shredded Gruyère cheese over the bread, covering the entire surface.

Broil Until Cheese is Melted and Browned:
- Place the bowls under the broiler until the cheese is melted, bubbly, and golden brown. Keep a close eye to prevent burning.

Serve Hot:
- Carefully remove the bowls from the broiler and serve the Gruyère French Onion Soup hot.

Enjoy:
- Enjoy the rich and flavorful Gruyère French Onion Soup with its gooey, golden cheese topping!

This Gruyère French Onion Soup is a comforting classic with sweet caramelized onions, savory broth, and a generous layer of melted Gruyère cheese. The toasty baguette slice adds a delightful crunch to every bite. Serve this hearty soup as a comforting meal on its own or as an elegant starter for a special dinner.

Feta Watermelon Salad

Ingredients:

- 4 cups seedless watermelon, cubed
- 1 cup feta cheese, crumbled
- 1/2 cup red onion, thinly sliced
- 1/4 cup fresh mint leaves, chopped
- 1/4 cup extra virgin olive oil
- 2 tablespoons balsamic glaze
- Salt and black pepper, to taste

Instructions:

Prepare Watermelon:
- Cut the seedless watermelon into bite-sized cubes, removing any seeds.

Combine Ingredients:
- In a large salad bowl, combine the watermelon cubes, crumbled feta cheese, thinly sliced red onion, and chopped fresh mint leaves.

Drizzle with Olive Oil:
- Drizzle extra virgin olive oil over the salad ingredients. The oil adds richness and complements the sweetness of the watermelon.

Season with Salt and Pepper:
- Season the salad with salt and black pepper to taste. Be mindful of the saltiness of the feta cheese.

Toss Gently:
- Gently toss the salad ingredients to ensure even distribution of flavors and dressing.

Drizzle with Balsamic Glaze:
- Drizzle balsamic glaze over the salad for a sweet and tangy finish. Adjust the amount based on your preference.

Chill (Optional):
- For a refreshing experience, you can chill the salad in the refrigerator for about 30 minutes before serving.

Serve:
- Serve the Feta Watermelon Salad in individual bowls or as a colorful side dish for a summer meal.

Enjoy:
- Enjoy the delightful combination of sweet watermelon, savory feta, and the burst of freshness from mint in this light and refreshing salad!

This Feta Watermelon Salad is a perfect balance of sweet and savory flavors, with the juicy sweetness of watermelon complemented by the saltiness of feta cheese. The addition of mint adds a refreshing element, while the balsamic glaze provides a sweet and tangy finish. It's a quick and easy salad that's perfect for summer gatherings or as a refreshing side dish.

Main Courses:

Four Cheese Pasta Bake

Ingredients:

- 1 pound (16 ounces) pasta (penne, rigatoni, or your choice)
- 2 cups marinara sauce
- 1 cup ricotta cheese
- 1 cup mozzarella cheese, shredded
- 1/2 cup Parmesan cheese, grated
- 1/2 cup fontina cheese, shredded
- 2 cloves garlic, minced
- 1 teaspoon dried oregano
- 1 teaspoon dried basil
- Salt and black pepper, to taste
- Fresh basil or parsley, chopped (for garnish)

Instructions:

Preheat the Oven:
- Preheat your oven to 375°F (190°C).

Cook Pasta:
- Cook the pasta according to the package instructions until al dente. Drain and set aside.

Prepare Cheeses:
- In a large mixing bowl, combine the ricotta, mozzarella, Parmesan, and fontina cheeses. Mix well.

Add Garlic and Herbs:
- Add minced garlic, dried oregano, and dried basil to the cheese mixture. Stir to incorporate the flavors.

Season with Salt and Pepper:
- Season the cheese mixture with salt and black pepper to taste. Adjust according to your preference.

Combine Pasta and Sauce:
- In a large mixing bowl, combine the cooked pasta and marinara sauce. Toss to coat the pasta evenly with the sauce.

Layer in Baking Dish:
- In a baking dish, layer half of the sauced pasta. Spread half of the cheese mixture evenly over the pasta.

Repeat Layers:
- Repeat the layers with the remaining sauced pasta and cheese mixture.

Bake in the Oven:
- Bake in the preheated oven for 25-30 minutes or until the cheese is melted and bubbly, and the top is golden brown.

Garnish and Serve:
- Remove from the oven and let it cool for a few minutes. Garnish with fresh basil or parsley.

Serve Hot:
- Serve the Four Cheese Pasta Bake hot, and enjoy the gooey, cheesy goodness!

This Four Cheese Pasta Bake is a decadent and comforting dish that combines the richness of four cheeses with savory marinara sauce and perfectly cooked pasta. It's a crowd-pleaser and an excellent option for a family dinner or when you're entertaining guests. The golden, bubbly cheese topping adds an irresistible touch to this indulgent pasta bake.

Grilled Cheese Sandwiches

Ingredients:

- 8 slices of your favorite bread (white, whole wheat, or sourdough)
- 8 ounces (about 2 cups) of your preferred cheese, sliced (cheddar, Swiss, mozzarella, or a combination)
- 4 tablespoons unsalted butter, softened
- Optional: Dijon mustard, mayonnaise, or pesto for spreading

Instructions:

Preheat the Griddle or Pan:
- Preheat a griddle or a non-stick skillet over medium heat.

Butter the Bread Slices:
- Spread a thin layer of softened butter on one side of each slice of bread.

Assemble the Sandwiches:
- Place the bread slices, buttered side down, on a clean surface. If desired, spread Dijon mustard, mayonnaise, or pesto on the unbuttered side of each slice.

Add Cheese Slices:
- Arrange the cheese slices on the bread slices. You can mix different types of cheese for a flavorful combination.

Top with Another Slice:
- Place another slice of bread on top, buttered side facing up.

Grill the Sandwiches:
- Carefully transfer the assembled sandwiches to the preheated griddle or skillet. Cook for 3-4 minutes on each side, or until the bread is golden brown, and the cheese is melted.

Press Down (Optional):
- If you want an extra crispy exterior, you can press down on the sandwiches with a spatula while cooking.

Serve Hot:
- Once both sides are golden brown, and the cheese is gooey, remove the grilled cheese sandwiches from the griddle or skillet.

Slice and Enjoy:
- Allow the sandwiches to cool for a minute before slicing them diagonally or into squares. Serve immediately and enjoy the melty goodness!

Variations (Optional):
- Get creative with your grilled cheese by adding ingredients like sliced tomatoes, bacon, caramelized onions, or avocado between the cheese layers.

Grilled Cheese Sandwiches are a classic comfort food that can be customized to suit your taste. Whether you prefer a simple cheddar melt or a gourmet combination, the key to a perfect grilled cheese is achieving a golden, crispy exterior and melty cheese on the inside. Serve with your favorite soup or enjoy on its own for a delicious and satisfying meal.

Chicken Alfredo Lasagna

Ingredients:

- 9 lasagna noodles, cooked according to package instructions
- 2 cups cooked chicken, shredded or diced
- 2 cups Alfredo sauce (store-bought or homemade)
- 2 cups rlcotta cheese
- 1 cup mozzarella cheese, shredded
- 1 cup Parmesan cheese, grated
- 1/2 cup fresh parsley, chopped
- 2 cloves garlic, minced
- 1 teaspoon dried oregano
- 1 teaspoon dried basil
- Salt and black pepper, to taste
- Cooking spray

Instructions:

Preheat the Oven:
- Preheat your oven to 375°F (190°C).

Prepare Alfredo Sauce:
- If making homemade Alfredo sauce, prepare it according to the recipe instructions.

Combine Chicken and Sauce:
- In a mixing bowl, combine the cooked chicken with the Alfredo sauce. Mix well to coat the chicken evenly.

Prepare Ricotta Mixture:
- In another bowl, mix the ricotta cheese, mozzarella cheese, Parmesan cheese, chopped parsley, minced garlic, dried oregano, dried basil, salt, and black pepper. Combine until well blended.

Assemble the Lasagna:
- Spray a baking dish with cooking spray. Spread a thin layer of the chicken Alfredo mixture on the bottom of the dish. Place three lasagna noodles on top.
- Spread a layer of the ricotta mixture over the noodles. Repeat the layers until all ingredients are used, finishing with a layer of the ricotta mixture on top.

Bake in the Oven:
- Cover the baking dish with aluminum foil and bake in the preheated oven for 25-30 minutes.

Remove Foil and Bake:
- Remove the foil and bake for an additional 10-15 minutes or until the top is golden brown and the lasagna is bubbly.

Let it Rest:
- Allow the Chicken Alfredo Lasagna to rest for 10 minutes before slicing.

Slice and Serve:
- Slice the lasagna into portions and serve hot. Garnish with additional parsley if desired.

Enjoy:
- Enjoy this creamy and flavorful Chicken Alfredo Lasagna as a comforting and satisfying meal!

This Chicken Alfredo Lasagna is a delightful twist on the traditional lasagna, featuring layers of tender chicken, creamy Alfredo sauce, and a cheesy ricotta mixture. It's a comforting and indulgent dish that's perfect for family dinners or special occasions. Serve it with a side salad for a complete and delicious meal.

Parmesan Crusted Chicken

Ingredients:

- 4 boneless, skinless chicken breasts
- 1 cup grated Parmesan cheese
- 1 cup breadcrumbs (plain or seasoned)
- 1 teaspoon garlic powder
- 1 teaspoon dried oregano
- 1 teaspoon dried basil
- Salt and black pepper, to taste
- 1/2 cup all-purpose flour
- 2 large eggs, beaten
- Cooking spray or olive oil

Instructions:

Preheat the Oven:
- Preheat your oven to 400°F (200°C).

Prepare Chicken:
- Pat the chicken breasts dry with paper towels. Season both sides with salt and black pepper.

Set Up Breading Station:
- In three separate shallow bowls, set up a breading station. Place flour in the first bowl, beaten eggs in the second bowl, and a mixture of Parmesan cheese, breadcrumbs, garlic powder, dried oregano, and dried basil in the third bowl.

Coat Chicken in Flour:
- Dredge each chicken breast in the flour, shaking off any excess.

Dip in Beaten Eggs:
- Dip the floured chicken into the beaten eggs, ensuring it is well coated.

Coat with Parmesan Mixture:
- Press the chicken into the Parmesan mixture, coating both sides evenly. Press the mixture onto the chicken to help it adhere.

Place on Baking Sheet:
- Place the breaded chicken breasts on a baking sheet lined with parchment paper or a greased baking dish.

Spray with Cooking Spray or Olive Oil:
- Lightly spray the top of each chicken breast with cooking spray or drizzle with olive oil. This helps to achieve a crispy crust.

Bake in the Oven:

- Bake in the preheated oven for 20-25 minutes or until the chicken reaches an internal temperature of 165°F (74°C) and the crust is golden brown and crispy.

Broil for Crispy Top (Optional):

- For an extra crispy top, you can broil the chicken for 1-2 minutes at the end of the cooking time. Keep a close eye to prevent burning.

Serve Hot:

- Remove the Parmesan Crusted Chicken from the oven and let it rest for a few minutes before serving.

Enjoy:

- Enjoy the delicious Parmesan Crusted Chicken with your favorite side dishes or a fresh salad!

This Parmesan Crusted Chicken is a flavorful and crispy dish that's simple to prepare. The combination of Parmesan cheese, breadcrumbs, and aromatic herbs creates a golden and savory crust, while the chicken remains juicy on the inside. It's a versatile recipe that pairs well with various sides, making it a family-friendly and satisfying meal.

Gnocchi with Gorgonzola Sauce

Ingredients:

- 1 pound (about 500g) potato gnocchi (store-bought or homemade)
- 1 cup Gorgonzola cheese, crumbled
- 1 cup heavy cream
- 1/2 cup grated Parmesan cheese
- 2 tablespoons unsalted butter
- Salt and black pepper, to taste
- Fresh parsley, chopped (for garnish)

Instructions:

Cook Gnocchi:
- Cook the potato gnocchi according to the package instructions or recipe. Drain and set aside.

Prepare Gorgonzola Sauce:
- In a saucepan over medium heat, melt the butter. Add the heavy cream and bring it to a gentle simmer.

Add Gorgonzola Cheese:
- Reduce the heat to low and stir in the crumbled Gorgonzola cheese. Continue stirring until the Gorgonzola is melted and the sauce is smooth.

Incorporate Parmesan Cheese:
- Add the grated Parmesan cheese to the sauce, stirring until it is fully incorporated and the sauce thickens slightly. Season with salt and black pepper to taste.

Combine with Gnocchi:
- Add the cooked gnocchi to the Gorgonzola sauce. Gently toss to coat the gnocchi evenly with the creamy sauce.

Serve Hot:
- Allow the Gnocchi with Gorgonzola Sauce to heat through. Once the gnocchi is coated and heated, remove the pan from heat.

Garnish and Serve:
- Garnish the dish with chopped fresh parsley for a burst of color and flavor.

Plate and Enjoy:
- Plate the Gnocchi with Gorgonzola Sauce and serve immediately. Enjoy the creamy and indulgent flavors!

This Gnocchi with Gorgonzola Sauce is a rich and satisfying pasta dish that combines soft potato gnocchi with a luxurious Gorgonzola cheese sauce. The creamy texture of the sauce and the bold flavor of Gorgonzola create a delicious and comforting meal. Serve it as a main course for a special dinner or enjoy it as a decadent side dish.

Sides and Snacks:

Cheese-Stuffed Jalapeños

Ingredients:

- 12 large jalapeño peppers
- 8 ounces cream cheese, softened
- 1 cup shredded cheddar cheese
- 1/2 cup cooked and crumbled bacon
- 2 green onions, finely chopped
- 1 teaspoon garlic powder
- 1/2 teaspoon onion powder
- 1/2 teaspoon smoked paprika (optional)
- Salt and black pepper, to taste
- Toothpicks (optional, for securing)

Instructions:

Preheat the Oven:
- Preheat your oven to 375°F (190°C).

Prepare Jalapeños:
- Cut jalapeños in half lengthwise, leaving the stems intact. Remove seeds and membranes for a milder flavor.

Prepare Filling:
- In a mixing bowl, combine softened cream cheese, shredded cheddar cheese, crumbled bacon, chopped green onions, garlic powder, onion powder, smoked paprika (if using), salt, and black pepper. Mix until well combined.

Stuff Jalapeños:
- Spoon the cheese mixture into each jalapeño half, pressing it down slightly to fill the cavity.

Secure with Toothpicks (Optional):
- If the jalapeños are large and the filling is overflowing, you can secure them with toothpicks by placing a toothpick through the center.

Arrange on Baking Sheet:
- Place the stuffed jalapeños on a baking sheet lined with parchment paper or a greased baking dish.

Bake in the Oven:
- Bake in the preheated oven for 20-25 minutes or until the jalapeños are tender, and the cheese is melted and bubbly.

Broil for Crispy Top (Optional):

- If you prefer a crispy top, you can broil the stuffed jalapeños for 1-2 minutes until the cheese is golden brown. Keep a close eye to prevent burning.

Serve Hot:

- Remove from the oven and let them cool slightly before serving.

Enjoy:

- Serve these Cheese-Stuffed Jalapeños as a flavorful appetizer or party snack. Enjoy the creamy and spicy combination!

These Cheese-Stuffed Jalapeños are a popular and irresistible appetizer that brings together the heat of jalapeños with a creamy and cheesy filling. The addition of bacon and green onions adds savory and smoky flavors, making them a crowd-pleaser at gatherings. Whether you're hosting a party or looking for a tasty snack, these stuffed jalapeños are sure to be a hit!

Truffle Mac and Cheese Bites

Ingredients:

- 2 cups elbow macaroni, cooked al dente
- 2 tablespoons truffle oil
- 3 tablespoons unsalted butter
- 3 tablespoons all-purpose flour
- 2 cups milk
- 2 cups sharp cheddar cheese, shredded
- 1 cup Gruyère cheese, shredded
- 1/2 cup Parmesan cheese, grated
- Salt and black pepper, to taste
- 1/4 teaspoon nutmeg, grated (optional)
- 1/2 cup breadcrumbs
- 2 tablespoons fresh parsley, chopped (for garnish)
- Cooking spray

Instructions:

Preheat the Oven:
- Preheat your oven to 375°F (190°C). Grease a mini muffin tin with cooking spray.

Cook Macaroni:
- Cook the elbow macaroni according to package instructions until al dente. Drain and set aside.

Prepare Truffle Mac and Cheese:
- In a large saucepan, heat truffle oil and butter over medium heat. Stir in the flour to create a roux, cooking for 1-2 minutes until it's a light golden color.
- Gradually whisk in the milk to avoid lumps. Cook, whisking constantly, until the mixture thickens.
- Reduce heat to low and add the shredded cheddar, Gruyère, and Parmesan cheeses. Stir until the cheeses are melted and the sauce is smooth.

Season the Sauce:
- Season the cheese sauce with salt, black pepper, and grated nutmeg (if using). Adjust the seasoning to taste.

Combine with Macaroni:
- Add the cooked macaroni to the cheese sauce, stirring until the macaroni is well coated.

Spoon into Mini Muffin Tin:

- Spoon the truffle mac and cheese mixture into the prepared mini muffin tin, pressing it down slightly.

Prepare Breadcrumbs:
- In a small bowl, combine breadcrumbs with a drizzle of truffle oil for added flavor.

Top with Breadcrumbs:
- Sprinkle the truffle-infused breadcrumbs over the tops of each mac and cheese bite.

Bake in the Oven:
- Bake in the preheated oven for 15-18 minutes or until the tops are golden brown and the bites are set.

Garnish and Serve:
- Remove from the oven and let the Truffle Mac and Cheese Bites cool for a few minutes. Garnish with chopped fresh parsley.

Serve Warm:
- Serve these delightful bites warm as an appetizer or a unique party snack.

Enjoy:
- Enjoy the luxurious flavors of truffle-infused mac and cheese in a bite-sized, irresistible form!

These Truffle Mac and Cheese Bites offer a gourmet twist on the classic comfort food. The truffle oil adds an extra layer of sophistication and earthy flavor to the creamy mac and cheese, making them perfect for special occasions or elegant gatherings. The individual bites make serving and enjoying this delicious dish even more convenient.

Truffle Mac and Cheese Bites

Ingredients:

- 2 cups elbow macaroni, cooked al dente
- 2 tablespoons truffle oil
- 3 tablespoons unsalted butter
- 3 tablespoons all-purpose flour
- 2 cups milk
- 2 cups sharp cheddar cheese, shredded
- 1 cup Gruyère cheese, shredded
- 1/2 cup Parmesan cheese, grated
- Salt and black pepper, to taste
- 1/4 teaspoon nutmeg, grated (optional)
- 1/2 cup breadcrumbs
- 2 tablespoons fresh parsley, chopped (for garnish)
- Cooking spray

Instructions:

Preheat the Oven:
- Preheat your oven to 375°F (190°C). Grease a mini muffin tin with cooking spray.

Cook Macaroni:
- Cook the elbow macaroni according to package instructions until al dente. Drain and set aside.

Prepare Truffle Mac and Cheese:
- In a large saucepan, heat truffle oil and butter over medium heat. Stir in the flour to create a roux, cooking for 1-2 minutes until it's a light golden color.
- Gradually whisk in the milk to avoid lumps. Cook, whisking constantly, until the mixture thickens.
- Reduce heat to low and add the shredded cheddar, Gruyère, and Parmesan cheeses. Stir until the cheeses are melted and the sauce is smooth.

Season the Sauce:
- Season the cheese sauce with salt, black pepper, and grated nutmeg (if using). Adjust the seasoning to taste.

Combine with Macaroni:
- Add the cooked macaroni to the cheese sauce, stirring until the macaroni is well coated.

Spoon into Mini Muffin Tin:

- Spoon the truffle mac and cheese mixture into the prepared mini muffin tin, pressing it down slightly.

Prepare Breadcrumbs:
- In a small bowl, combine breadcrumbs with a drizzle of truffle oil for added flavor.

Top with Breadcrumbs:
- Sprinkle the truffle-infused breadcrumbs over the tops of each mac and cheese bite.

Bake in the Oven:
- Bake in the preheated oven for 15-18 minutes or until the tops are golden brown and the bites are set.

Garnish and Serve:
- Remove from the oven and let the Truffle Mac and Cheese Bites cool for a few minutes. Garnish with chopped fresh parsley.

Serve Warm:
- Serve these delightful bites warm as an appetizer or a unique party snack.

Enjoy:
- Enjoy the luxurious flavors of truffle-infused mac and cheese in a bite-sized, irresistible form!

These Truffle Mac and Cheese Bites offer a gourmet twist on the classic comfort food. The truffle oil adds an extra layer of sophistication and earthy flavor to the creamy mac and cheese, making them perfect for special occasions or elegant gatherings. The individual bites make serving and enjoying this delicious dish even more convenient.

Cheese Twists

Ingredients:

- 1 sheet puff pastry, thawed
- 1 cup shredded cheddar cheese
- 1/4 cup grated Parmesan cheese
- 1 teaspoon garlic powder
- 1 teaspoon dried oregano
- 1/2 teaspoon paprika
- 1 large egg, beaten (for egg wash)
- Sesame seeds or poppy seeds (optional, for topping)

Instructions:

Preheat the Oven:
- Preheat your oven to 400°F (200°C). Line a baking sheet with parchment paper.

Roll Out Puff Pastry:
- Roll out the thawed puff pastry sheet on a lightly floured surface to smooth out any creases.

Combine Cheeses and Seasonings:
- In a bowl, mix together shredded cheddar cheese, grated Parmesan cheese, garlic powder, dried oregano, and paprika.

Spread Cheese Mixture:
- Spread the cheese mixture evenly over the entire surface of the puff pastry sheet.

Fold and Press:
- Fold the puff pastry sheet in half, covering the cheese mixture. Press down gently to secure the layers.

Cut into Strips:
- Using a sharp knife or a pizza cutter, cut the pastry into strips, about 1/2 to 1 inch wide.

Twist Each Strip:
- Take each strip and twist it a few times. Place the twisted strips on the prepared baking sheet, leaving space between each.

Brush with Egg Wash:
- Brush the twisted strips with the beaten egg. This gives them a golden and shiny finish.

Optional: Sprinkle Seeds:
- If desired, sprinkle sesame seeds or poppy seeds over the twisted strips for added texture and flavor.

Bake in the Oven:

- Bake in the preheated oven for 12-15 minutes or until the cheese twists are puffed and golden brown.

Cool and Serve:

- Allow the cheese twists to cool for a few minutes before serving.

Enjoy:

- Serve these Cheese Twists as a delightful appetizer or snack. Enjoy the cheesy, flaky goodness!

These Cheese Twists are a simple and delicious snack that combines the flakiness of puff pastry with the savory goodness of cheddar and Parmesan cheeses. The addition of garlic, oregano, and paprika adds a flavorful kick. These twists are perfect for entertaining guests or as a tasty treat for yourself. They're quick to make and disappear even faster!

Loaded Nachos with Queso

Ingredients:

- 1 bag (about 10 ounces) tortilla chips
- 2 cups shredded cheddar cheese
- 1 cup shredded Monterey Jack cheese
- 1 cup black beans, drained and rinsed
- 1 cup corn kernels (fresh or thawed if frozen)
- 1 cup cherry tomatoes, halved
- 1/2 cup sliced black olives
- 1/2 cup pickled jalapeño slices
- 1/4 cup chopped fresh cilantro
- 1/4 cup diced red onion
- Sour cream, for drizzling
- Guacamole, for serving (optional)
- Salsa, for serving (optional)

Queso Ingredients:

- 1 tablespoon unsalted butter
- 1 tablespoon all-purpose flour
- 1 cup whole milk
- 2 cups shredded sharp cheddar cheese
- 1/2 teaspoon garlic powder
- 1/2 teaspoon onion powder
- 1/4 teaspoon cayenne pepper (optional)
- Salt and black pepper, to taste

Instructions:

Preheat the Oven:
- Preheat your oven to 375°F (190°C).

Prepare Queso Sauce:
- In a saucepan over medium heat, melt butter. Stir in flour to create a roux. Gradually whisk in the milk until smooth.
- Add shredded cheddar cheese, garlic powder, onion powder, cayenne pepper (if using), salt, and black pepper. Stir continuously until the cheese is fully melted and the sauce is smooth. Remove from heat.

Assemble Nachos:
- Arrange the tortilla chips on a large baking sheet in a single layer.

- Sprinkle shredded cheddar and Monterey Jack cheeses evenly over the tortilla chips.
- Distribute black beans, corn, cherry tomatoes, black olives, jalapeño slices, and red onion evenly over the cheese-covered chips.

Bake in the Oven:
- Bake the loaded nachos in the preheated oven for about 10-12 minutes or until the cheese is melted and bubbly.

Drizzle with Queso:
- Drizzle the prepared queso sauce over the loaded nachos. Use as much or as little as you desire.

Garnish:
- Sprinkle chopped cilantro over the nachos for a burst of freshness.

Serve Hot:
- Drizzle sour cream over the top and serve the loaded nachos hot.

Optional: Serve with Guacamole and Salsa:
- Serve with guacamole and salsa on the side if desired.

Enjoy:
- Enjoy these Loaded Nachos with Queso as a delicious appetizer, game-day snack, or a crowd-pleasing party dish!

These Loaded Nachos with Queso are a crowd-pleaser, combining crispy tortilla chips with melted cheese, beans, veggies, and a flavorful queso sauce. Whether you're hosting a gathering or just craving a tasty snack, these nachos are easy to make and always a hit. Customize the toppings to your liking, and don't forget the drizzle of creamy queso for the perfect finish!

Baked Goat Cheese and Tomato Dip

Ingredients:

- 8 ounces goat cheese, softened
- 1 cup cherry tomatoes, halved
- 2 cloves garlic, minced
- 2 tablespoons extra-virgin olive oil
- 1 tablespoon balsamic vinegar
- 1 tablespoon fresh basil, chopped
- 1 teaspoon dried oregano
- Salt and black pepper, to taste
- Baguette slices or crackers, for serving

Instructions:

Preheat the Oven:
- Preheat your oven to 375°F (190°C).

Prepare Goat Cheese:
- In a mixing bowl, combine the softened goat cheese with minced garlic. Mix until well combined.

Spread Goat Cheese in Baking Dish:
- Spread the goat cheese mixture evenly in a baking dish or a small ovenproof skillet.

Top with Tomatoes:
- Arrange the halved cherry tomatoes over the goat cheese.

Drizzle with Olive Oil and Balsamic Vinegar:
- Drizzle extra-virgin olive oil and balsamic vinegar over the tomatoes and goat cheese.

Season with Herbs:
- Sprinkle chopped fresh basil and dried oregano over the top. Season with salt and black pepper to taste.

Bake in the Oven:
- Bake in the preheated oven for 20-25 minutes or until the goat cheese is bubbly, and the tomatoes are roasted.

Broil for Golden Top (Optional):
- If you desire a golden top, you can broil the dip for an additional 2-3 minutes, keeping a close eye to prevent burning.

Remove from Oven:
- Remove the baked goat cheese and tomato dip from the oven.

Serve Warm:
- Serve the dip warm with baguette slices or crackers.

Enjoy:
- Enjoy this delightful Baked Goat Cheese and Tomato Dip as a flavorful and savory appetizer!

This Baked Goat Cheese and Tomato Dip is a simple and elegant appetizer that brings together the creamy richness of goat cheese with the sweet and tangy flavors of roasted cherry tomatoes. The addition of garlic, balsamic vinegar, and herbs enhances the overall taste, making it a perfect dish for entertaining or enjoying a cozy night in. Serve it with crusty bread or crackers for a delicious and satisfying experience.

Pizza and Flatbreads:

Margherita Pizza

Ingredients:

- Pizza dough (store-bought or homemade)
- 1/2 cup pizza sauce
- 8 ounces fresh mozzarella cheese, sliced
- 2 large tomatoes, thinly sliced
- Fresh basil leaves
- Extra-virgin olive oil
- Salt and black pepper, to taste
- Cornmeal or flour, for dusting

Instructions:

Preheat the Oven:
- Preheat your oven to the highest temperature it can go (usually around 475-500°F or 245-260°C). If you have a pizza stone, place it in the oven to heat.

Prepare Pizza Dough:
- Roll out the pizza dough on a lightly floured surface. If using a pizza stone, you can also stretch the dough on a piece of parchment paper.

Dust with Cornmeal or Flour:
- If using a pizza stone, sprinkle cornmeal or flour on a pizza peel to prevent sticking. If you don't have a pizza stone, you can use a baking sheet.

Spread Pizza Sauce:
- Spread the pizza sauce evenly over the rolled-out dough, leaving a small border around the edges for the crust.

Arrange Mozzarella Slices:
- Place the fresh mozzarella slices evenly on top of the sauce.

Add Tomato Slices:
- Arrange the thinly sliced tomatoes on the pizza.

Season with Salt and Pepper:
- Season the pizza with a pinch of salt and black pepper to taste.

Bake in the Oven:
- If using a pizza stone, carefully transfer the pizza (on the parchment paper) onto the preheated stone in the oven. If using a baking sheet, place the sheet directly in the oven.
- Bake for about 10-12 minutes or until the crust is golden and the cheese is melted and bubbly.

Add Fresh Basil:

- Remove the pizza from the oven and immediately sprinkle fresh basil leaves on top.

Drizzle with Olive Oil:

- Drizzle extra-virgin olive oil over the pizza for added flavor.

Slice and Serve:

- Allow the Margherita Pizza to cool for a few minutes before slicing. Serve hot.

Enjoy:

- Enjoy this classic Margherita Pizza with its simple and delicious flavors!

This Margherita Pizza celebrates the classic combination of fresh tomatoes, mozzarella, and basil. The key to a perfect Margherita is using high-quality, fresh ingredients. Whether you're making it for a casual dinner or a gathering, this pizza is sure to be a crowd-pleaser!

Pear and Gorgonzola Flatbread

Ingredients:

- 1 store-bought flatbread or pizza crust
- 2 tablespoons olive oil
- 1 cup Gorgonzola cheese, crumbled
- 2 ripe pears, thinly sliced
- 1/2 cup walnuts, chopped
- 2 tablespoons honey
- Fresh arugula, for garnish (optional)
- Balsamic glaze, for drizzling (optional)
- Salt and black pepper, to taste

Instructions:

Preheat the Oven:
- Preheat your oven according to the instructions on the flatbread or pizza crust packaging.

Prepare Flatbread:
- If using a store-bought flatbread, place it on a baking sheet lined with parchment paper. If using pizza dough, roll it out on a floured surface to your desired thickness.

Brush with Olive Oil:
- Brush the flatbread with olive oil, ensuring an even coating.

Spread Gorgonzola:
- Sprinkle crumbled Gorgonzola cheese evenly over the flatbread.

Add Pear Slices:
- Arrange thinly sliced pears over the Gorgonzola.

Scatter Chopped Walnuts:
- Scatter chopped walnuts over the flatbread.

Season with Salt and Pepper:
- Season the flatbread with a pinch of salt and black pepper to taste.

Bake in the Oven:
- Bake in the preheated oven according to the flatbread or pizza crust instructions, typically for 10-15 minutes or until the edges are golden and the cheese is melted.

Drizzle with Honey:
- Remove the flatbread from the oven and drizzle honey over the top.

Optional: Garnish with Arugula:

- For added freshness, you can garnish the flatbread with fresh arugula.

Optional: Drizzle with Balsamic Glaze:

- If desired, drizzle with balsamic glaze for an extra burst of flavor.

Slice and Serve:

- Allow the Pear and Gorgonzola Flatbread to cool for a few minutes before slicing.

Enjoy:

- Enjoy this delightful and savory-sweet flatbread as a light meal or appetizer!

This Pear and Gorgonzola Flatbread offers a perfect balance of sweet and savory flavors, making it a sophisticated yet easy-to-make dish. The combination of juicy pears, creamy Gorgonzola, and crunchy walnuts creates a delightful texture and taste. Serve it as a light lunch, appetizer, or even as a unique addition to your next gathering.

Buffalo Chicken Pizza

Ingredients:

- 1 store-bought pizza crust or pizza dough
- 1/2 cup buffalo sauce (adjust to taste)
- 1 cup cooked and shredded chicken breast
- 1 cup shredded mozzarella cheese
- 1/2 cup crumbled blue cheese
- 1/4 cup thinly sliced red onion
- 2 tablespoons chopped fresh cilantro (optional)
- Ranch or blue cheese dressing, for drizzling (optional)
- Celery sticks, for serving (optional)

Instructions:

Preheat the Oven:
- Preheat your oven according to the instructions on the pizza crust or dough packaging.

Prepare Pizza Crust:
- If using a store-bought pizza crust, place it on a baking sheet. If using pizza dough, roll it out on a floured surface to your desired thickness.

Toss Chicken in Buffalo Sauce:
- In a bowl, toss the cooked and shredded chicken in buffalo sauce until well coated.

Spread Buffalo Chicken:
- Spread the buffalo sauced chicken evenly over the pizza crust.

Sprinkle with Mozzarella:
- Sprinkle shredded mozzarella cheese over the buffalo chicken.

Add Blue Cheese and Red Onion:
- Scatter crumbled blue cheese and thinly sliced red onion over the pizza.

Bake in the Oven:
- Bake in the preheated oven according to the pizza crust or dough instructions, usually for 10-15 minutes or until the crust is golden and the cheese is melted and bubbly.

Optional: Drizzle with Dressing:
- If desired, drizzle ranch or blue cheese dressing over the top for added flavor.

Optional: Garnish with Cilantro:
- Garnish the pizza with chopped fresh cilantro for a burst of freshness.

Slice and Serve:
- Allow the Buffalo Chicken Pizza to cool for a few minutes before slicing.

Optional: Serve with Celery Sticks:
- For an authentic buffalo chicken experience, serve the pizza with celery sticks on the side.

Enjoy:
- Enjoy this delicious Buffalo Chicken Pizza with its spicy, tangy, and savory flavors!

This Buffalo Chicken Pizza is a perfect combination of the classic buffalo chicken flavors in a pizza form. The spicy buffalo sauce, tender chicken, melted cheeses, and crisp crust create a mouthwatering dish that's perfect for game days, parties, or a satisfying weeknight dinner. Customize the toppings to your liking and enjoy the bold and delicious taste!

Mushroom and Fontina Flatbread

Ingredients:

- 1 store-bought flatbread or pizza crust
- 2 tablespoons olive oil
- 2 cups mixed mushrooms (such as cremini, shiitake, or oyster), sliced
- 2 cloves garlic, minced
- Salt and black pepper, to taste
- 1 cup shredded Fontina cheese
- 1/4 cup freshly grated Parmesan cheese
- Fresh thyme leaves, for garnish
- Truffle oil (optional, for drizzling)
- Arugula, for serving (optional)

Instructions:

Preheat the Oven:
- Preheat your oven according to the instructions on the flatbread or pizza crust packaging.

Prepare Flatbread:
- If using a store-bought flatbread, place it on a baking sheet lined with parchment paper. If using pizza dough, roll it out on a floured surface to your desired thickness.

Sauté Mushrooms:
- In a skillet, heat olive oil over medium heat. Add sliced mushrooms and minced garlic. Sauté until the mushrooms are golden brown and the moisture has evaporated. Season with salt and black pepper to taste.

Spread Mushrooms on Flatbread:
- Spread the sautéed mushrooms evenly over the flatbread.

Sprinkle with Cheeses:
- Sprinkle shredded Fontina cheese and freshly grated Parmesan cheese over the mushrooms.

Bake in the Oven:
- Bake in the preheated oven according to the flatbread or pizza crust instructions, typically for 10-15 minutes or until the crust is golden and the cheeses are melted.

Garnish with Thyme:
- Remove the flatbread from the oven and sprinkle fresh thyme leaves over the top.

Optional: Drizzle with Truffle Oil:

- For an extra layer of flavor, drizzle truffle oil over the flatbread.

Optional: Serve with Arugula:

- For freshness, you can serve the flatbread with a handful of arugula on top.

Slice and Serve:

- Allow the Mushroom and Fontina Flatbread to cool for a few minutes before slicing.

Enjoy:

- Enjoy this savory and sophisticated flatbread as a delightful appetizer or light meal!

This Mushroom and Fontina Flatbread offers a combination of earthy mushrooms, melted Fontina and Parmesan cheeses, and aromatic thyme for a rich and flavorful experience. The truffle oil, if used, adds a touch of luxury to the dish. Serve it as an appetizer for gatherings or enjoy it as a satisfying lunch or dinner option. Customize the toppings and make it your own!

Prosciutto and Fig Pizza

Ingredients:

- 1 store-bought pizza crust or pizza dough
- 2 tablespoons olive oil
- 1 cup fresh figs, sliced
- 4 ounces prosciutto, thinly sliced
- 1 cup fresh mozzarella cheese, torn into pieces
- 1/4 cup crumbled goat cheese
- Balsamic glaze, for drizzling
- Fresh arugula, for garnish
- Salt and black pepper, to taste

Instructions:

Preheat the Oven:
- Preheat your oven according to the instructions on the pizza crust or dough packaging.

Prepare Pizza Crust:
- If using a store-bought pizza crust, place it on a baking sheet. If using pizza dough, roll it out on a floured surface to your desired thickness.

Brush with Olive Oil:
- Brush the pizza crust with olive oil, ensuring an even coating.

Arrange Figs and Prosciutto:
- Scatter the sliced fresh figs and thinly sliced prosciutto evenly over the pizza crust.

Add Fresh Mozzarella:
- Tuck torn pieces of fresh mozzarella among the figs and prosciutto.

Sprinkle with Goat Cheese:
- Sprinkle crumbled goat cheese over the pizza.

Season with Salt and Pepper:
- Season the pizza with a pinch of salt and black pepper to taste.

Bake in the Oven:
- Bake in the preheated oven according to the pizza crust or dough instructions, usually for 10-15 minutes or until the crust is golden and the cheese is melted and bubbly.

Drizzle with Balsamic Glaze:
- Remove the pizza from the oven and drizzle balsamic glaze over the top.

Garnish with Arugula:

- Garnish the pizza with fresh arugula for a peppery contrast.

Slice and Serve:

- Allow the Prosciutto and Fig Pizza to cool for a few minutes before slicing.

Enjoy:

- Enjoy this elegant and flavorful pizza with the perfect balance of sweet figs, salty prosciutto, and creamy cheeses!

This Prosciutto and Fig Pizza offers a delightful combination of sweet and savory flavors that make it a sophisticated and delicious option for any occasion. The addition of balsamic glaze and fresh arugula adds a finishing touch to this gourmet pizza. Serve it as an appetizer or main dish, and savor the unique blend of ingredients!

Desserts:

Cheesecake with Raspberry Coulis

Ingredients:

For the Cheesecake:

- 2 cups graham cracker crumbs
- 1/2 cup unsalted butter, melted
- 4 packages (32 ounces) cream cheese, softened
- 1 1/4 cups granulated sugar
- 4 large eggs
- 1 cup sour cream
- 1 teaspoon vanilla extract
- Zest of one lemon (optional)

For the Raspberry Coulis:

- 2 cups fresh or frozen raspberries
- 1/2 cup granulated sugar
- 1 tablespoon lemon juice

Instructions:

For the Cheesecake:

Preheat the Oven:
- Preheat your oven to 325°F (163°C). Grease a 9-inch springform pan with butter or cooking spray.

Prepare the Crust:
- In a bowl, combine the graham cracker crumbs and melted butter. Press the mixture firmly into the bottom of the prepared springform pan to create the crust.

Bake the Crust:
- Bake the crust in the preheated oven for 10 minutes. Remove from the oven and let it cool while you prepare the filling.

Prepare the Filling:
- In a large mixing bowl, beat the softened cream cheese until smooth and creamy. Add the granulated sugar and continue beating until well combined.

- Add the eggs one at a time, beating well after each addition. Add the sour cream, vanilla extract, and lemon zest (if using). Mix until the batter is smooth.

Pour into the Pan:
- Pour the cream cheese filling over the baked crust in the springform pan.

Bake the Cheesecake:
- Bake in the preheated oven for 50-60 minutes or until the center is set and the top is lightly browned.

Cool and Refrigerate:
- Allow the cheesecake to cool in the pan for about 1 hour, then refrigerate for at least 4 hours or overnight to firm up.

For the Raspberry Coulis:

Prepare the Coulis:
- In a saucepan, combine the raspberries, granulated sugar, and lemon juice. Cook over medium heat, stirring occasionally, until the raspberries break down and the mixture thickens slightly.

Strain the Coulis:
- Strain the raspberry mixture through a fine-mesh sieve to remove seeds and obtain a smooth coulis.

Cool:
- Let the raspberry coulis cool to room temperature.

Serve:
- Once the cheesecake has set and is chilled, slice and serve with a drizzle of raspberry coulis over each piece.

Enjoy:
- Enjoy this delightful Cheesecake with Raspberry Coulis as a sweet and tangy treat!

This Cheesecake with Raspberry Coulis is a perfect combination of rich, creamy cheesecake and the bright, fruity flavor of raspberry coulis. The smooth and velvety texture of the cheesecake pairs wonderfully with the vibrant and slightly tart raspberry sauce. It's a classic dessert that's sure to impress!

Chocolate Fondue with Assorted Dippers

Ingredients:

For the Chocolate Fondue:

- 8 ounces (about 1 1/3 cups) high-quality dark chocolate, chopped
- 1 cup heavy cream
- 2 tablespoons unsalted butter
- 1 teaspoon vanilla extract
- Pinch of salt

Assorted Dippers:

- Strawberries, washed and hulled
- Bananas, sliced
- Pineapple chunks
- Pretzel rods or pretzel twists
- Marshmallows
- Rice Krispies treats, cut into squares
- Pound cake or angel food cake, cut into cubes
- Dried apricots or figs
- Cookies, such as biscotti or shortbread

Instructions:

For the Chocolate Fondue:

Prepare the Chocolate:
- Place the chopped dark chocolate in a heatproof bowl.

Heat the Cream:
- In a saucepan over medium heat, heat the heavy cream until it just starts to simmer. Do not boil.

Pour Over Chocolate:
- Pour the hot cream over the chopped chocolate. Let it sit for a minute to soften the chocolate.

Stir Until Smooth:
- Stir the chocolate and cream mixture until smooth and well combined.

Add Butter and Vanilla:

- Add the unsalted butter, vanilla extract, and a pinch of salt to the chocolate mixture. Stir until the butter is melted and the fondue is smooth.

Transfer to Fondue Pot:
- Transfer the chocolate fondue to a fondue pot or a heatproof bowl that can be placed over a fondue burner.

Keep Warm:
- Keep the chocolate fondue warm over a low flame or with a fondue warmer.

Assorted Dippers:

Prepare Dippers:
- Wash, cut, and arrange the assorted dippers on a serving platter.

Serve:
- Invite guests to skewer their favorite dippers and dip them into the warm chocolate fondue.

Enjoy:
- Enjoy the indulgent experience of Chocolate Fondue with a variety of delicious dippers!

This Chocolate Fondue with Assorted Dippers is a fun and interactive dessert perfect for gatherings or special occasions. The rich and velvety chocolate pairs wonderfully with a variety of dippers, allowing everyone to customize their fondue experience. Whether it's a romantic evening or a family celebration, chocolate fondue is sure to be a crowd-pleaser!

Ricotta and Honey Tart

Ingredients:

For the Tart Crust:

- 1 1/2 cups all-purpose flour
- 1/2 cup unsalted butter, cold and diced
- 1/4 cup granulated sugar
- 1/4 teaspoon salt
- 1 large egg, beaten

For the Filling:

- 2 cups ricotta cheese
- 1/2 cup confectioners' sugar
- 1 teaspoon vanilla extract
- Zest of one lemon
- 2 large eggs

For Assembly and Garnish:

- Honey, for drizzling
- Fresh berries (strawberries, blueberries, or raspberries), for garnish
- Mint leaves, for garnish (optional)

Instructions:

For the Tart Crust:

Preheat the Oven:
- Preheat your oven to 375°F (190°C).

Prepare Tart Crust:
- In a food processor, combine the flour, cold diced butter, granulated sugar, and salt. Pulse until the mixture resembles coarse crumbs.

Add Egg:
- Add the beaten egg and pulse just until the dough comes together.

Form Dough:
- Turn the dough out onto a floured surface and knead it briefly to bring it together. Form it into a disk, wrap in plastic wrap, and refrigerate for at least 30 minutes.

Roll Out and Line Tart Pan:

- On a floured surface, roll out the chilled dough to fit a tart pan. Press the dough into the bottom and up the sides of the tart pan. Trim any excess dough.

Prebake the Crust:

- Line the tart crust with parchment paper and fill it with pie weights or dried beans. Bake in the preheated oven for about 15 minutes. Remove the weights and parchment paper, then bake for an additional 5-7 minutes or until the crust is golden. Allow it to cool while preparing the filling.

For the Filling:

Prepare Ricotta Filling:

- In a mixing bowl, combine ricotta cheese, confectioners' sugar, vanilla extract, lemon zest, and eggs. Mix until well combined and smooth.

For Assembly:

Fill the Tart:

- Pour the ricotta filling into the prebaked tart crust and spread it evenly.

Bake:

- Bake in the oven for 25-30 minutes or until the filling is set and has a slight golden color.

Cool:

- Allow the tart to cool completely before serving.

Drizzle with Honey and Garnish:

- Just before serving, drizzle honey over the top of the tart. Garnish with fresh berries and mint leaves if desired.

Slice and Serve:

- Slice the Ricotta and Honey Tart into wedges and serve.

Enjoy:

- Enjoy this delightful Ricotta and Honey Tart with its creamy filling and sweet honey drizzle!

This Ricotta and Honey Tart is a light and luscious dessert that combines the richness of ricotta with the sweetness of honey. The lemon zest adds a refreshing zing, and the fresh berries provide a burst of fruity goodness. It's a perfect treat for a special occasion or a sweet ending to a meal.

Blueberry Cheesecake Bars

Ingredients:

For the Crust:

- 1 1/2 cups graham cracker crumbs
- 1/3 cup unsalted butter, melted
- 1/4 cup granulated sugar

For the Cheesecake Filling:

- 16 ounces (2 packages) cream cheese, softened
- 1/2 cup granulated sugar
- 2 large eggs
- 1 teaspoon vanilla extract
- 1/4 cup sour cream

For the Blueberry Topping:

- 1 1/2 cups fresh or frozen blueberries
- 1/4 cup granulated sugar
- 1 tablespoon cornstarch
- 1/4 cup water
- 1 tablespoon lemon juice

Instructions:

For the Crust:

Preheat the Oven:
- Preheat your oven to 325°F (163°C). Line a 9x9-inch baking pan with parchment paper, leaving an overhang on two sides for easy removal.

Make the Crust:
- In a bowl, combine the graham cracker crumbs, melted butter, and granulated sugar. Press the mixture firmly into the bottom of the prepared pan to form the crust.

Bake the Crust:
- Bake the crust in the preheated oven for about 10 minutes or until set. Remove from the oven and let it cool slightly while you prepare the filling.

For the Cheesecake Filling:

Prepare Cheesecake Filling:

- In a large mixing bowl, beat the softened cream cheese until smooth. Add the granulated sugar and beat until well combined.

Add Eggs and Vanilla:

- Add the eggs one at a time, beating well after each addition. Mix in the vanilla extract.

Incorporate Sour Cream:

- Fold in the sour cream until the batter is smooth and creamy.

For the Blueberry Topping:

Prepare Blueberry Topping:

- In a saucepan, combine the blueberries, granulated sugar, cornstarch, water, and lemon juice.

Cook Blueberry Mixture:

- Cook over medium heat, stirring frequently until the mixture thickens and the blueberries burst, releasing their juices. This usually takes about 5-7 minutes.

Assemble and Bake:

- Pour the cream cheese filling over the baked crust, spreading it evenly. Spoon the blueberry topping over the cream cheese layer.

Bake Until Set:

- Bake in the preheated oven for 30-35 minutes or until the edges are set, and the center is slightly jiggly.

Cool and Refrigerate:

- Allow the Blueberry Cheesecake Bars to cool in the pan, then refrigerate for at least 3 hours or until fully chilled.

Slice and Serve:

- Use the parchment paper overhang to lift the bars from the pan. Slice into squares and serve.

Enjoy:

- Enjoy these luscious Blueberry Cheesecake Bars as a delightful treat!

These Blueberry Cheesecake Bars are a perfect combination of creamy cheesecake, sweet blueberry topping, and a buttery graham cracker crust. They're great for parties, potlucks, or simply satisfying your sweet tooth. The vibrant blueberry layer adds a burst of flavor to every bite!

Cheddar Apple Pie

Ingredients:

For the Pie Crust:

- 2 1/2 cups all-purpose flour
- 1 cup unsalted butter, cold and cubed
- 1 teaspoon salt
- 1 tablespoon granulated sugar
- 1/2 cup sharp cheddar cheese, shredded
- Ice water (about 1/4 to 1/2 cup)

For the Apple Filling:

- 6 cups apples, peeled, cored, and thinly sliced (a mix of sweet and tart varieties like Granny Smith and Honeycrisp)
- 3/4 cup granulated sugar
- 1/4 cup brown sugar, packed
- 1 teaspoon ground cinnamon
- 1/4 teaspoon ground nutmeg
- 1/4 teaspoon salt
- 2 tablespoons lemon juice
- 3 tablespoons cornstarch

For Assembly:

- 1 cup sharp cheddar cheese, shredded
- 1 tablespoon unsalted butter, cut into small pieces
- 1 tablespoon granulated sugar (for sprinkling)

Instructions:

For the Pie Crust:

Prepare the Pie Crust:
- In a food processor, combine the flour, cold cubed butter, salt, and sugar. Pulse until the mixture resembles coarse crumbs.

Add Cheddar Cheese:

- Add the shredded cheddar cheese to the mixture and pulse briefly to combine.

Add Ice Water:
- With the food processor running, gradually add ice water, one tablespoon at a time, until the dough just begins to come together.

Form Dough:
- Turn the dough out onto a floured surface and knead it briefly to bring it together. Divide the dough into two equal portions, shape each into a disk, wrap in plastic wrap, and refrigerate for at least 1 hour.

For the Apple Filling:

Prepare Apple Filling:
- In a large mixing bowl, combine the sliced apples, granulated sugar, brown sugar, cinnamon, nutmeg, salt, lemon juice, and cornstarch. Toss until the apples are evenly coated.

For Assembly:

Preheat the Oven:
- Preheat your oven to 375°F (190°C).

Roll Out Pie Crust:
- On a floured surface, roll out one disk of pie crust to fit a 9-inch pie dish. Place it in the dish, trim any excess, and flute the edges.

Add Cheese Layer:
- Sprinkle half of the shredded cheddar cheese over the bottom of the pie crust.

Fill with Apple Mixture:
- Spoon the prepared apple filling over the cheese layer.

Top with Cheese and Butter:
- Sprinkle the remaining cheddar cheese over the apple filling. Dot the filling with small pieces of butter.

Roll Out Top Crust:
- Roll out the second disk of pie crust and place it over the apple filling. Trim and crimp the edges to seal the pie.

Cut Slits:
- Use a sharp knife to cut slits or create a decorative pattern on the top crust for steam to escape.

Sprinkle with Sugar:

- Sprinkle the top crust with granulated sugar for a golden finish.

Bake:
- Place the pie on a baking sheet to catch any drips and bake in the preheated oven for 50-60 minutes or until the crust is golden and the filling is bubbling.

Cool:
- Allow the Cheddar Apple Pie to cool for at least 3 hours before slicing.

Enjoy:
- Enjoy this unique twist on classic apple pie with a delightful cheddar cheese layer!

This Cheddar Apple Pie combines the sweet and spiced apple filling with the savory sharpness of cheddar cheese, creating a deliciously balanced and flavorful dessert. The flaky crust, gooey cheese, and tender apples make each bite a delightful experience. Serve it warm with a scoop of vanilla ice cream for an extra treat!

Breakfast:

Cheese and Herb Omelette

Ingredients:

- 3 large eggs
- Salt and pepper, to taste
- 1 tablespoon butter or cooking oil
- 1/4 cup shredded cheddar cheese (or your favorite cheese)
- 1 tablespoon fresh herbs (such as chives, parsley, or thyme), chopped

Optional Add-ins:

- Diced tomatoes
- Sautéed mushrooms
- Spinach leaves
- Diced bell peppers
- Cooked ham or bacon

Instructions:

Prepare Ingredients:
- Crack the eggs into a bowl and whisk them together. Season with salt and pepper. Chop the fresh herbs.

Heat Pan:
- Place a non-stick skillet over medium heat and add butter or cooking oil. Allow it to melt and coat the bottom of the pan.

Pour Eggs into Pan:
- Pour the whisked eggs into the heated pan, swirling to ensure an even distribution.

Cook Base of Omelette:
- Let the eggs cook undisturbed for a minute or two until the edges start to set.

Add Cheese and Herbs:
- Sprinkle the shredded cheddar cheese and chopped herbs over one-half of the omelette.

Optional Add-ins:
- If desired, add any optional ingredients like diced tomatoes, sautéed mushrooms, spinach, bell peppers, or cooked ham/bacon on top of the cheese and herbs.

Fold the Omelette:
- Once the edges of the omelette are set and the center is still slightly runny, use a spatula to carefully fold the omelette in half, covering the cheese and fillings.

Finish Cooking:
- Allow the omelette to cook for an additional 1-2 minutes until the cheese melts, and the center is fully cooked but still moist.

Slide onto Plate:
- Carefully slide the omelette onto a plate, folding it as it exits the pan.

Garnish and Serve:
- Garnish with additional fresh herbs if desired. Serve the Cheese and Herb Omelette hot.

Enjoy:
- Enjoy this flavorful and cheesy omelette for a delicious and satisfying breakfast or brunch!

Feel free to customize this Cheese and Herb Omelette with your favorite ingredients and experiment with different cheese and herb combinations. It's a versatile and quick meal that can be tailored to your taste preferences.

Cheese and Spinach Breakfast Casserole

Ingredients:

- 8 large eggs
- 1 1/2 cups milk
- 1 teaspoon Dijon mustard
- Salt and pepper, to taste
- 8 slices of bread, cubed (day-old or slightly stale works well)
- 1 1/2 cups shredded cheddar cheese
- 1 1/2 cups fresh spinach, chopped
- 1/2 cup diced ham or cooked sausage (optional)
- 1/4 cup diced onions (optional)
- 1/4 cup diced bell peppers (optional)
- 2 tablespoons butter, melted
- Fresh parsley or chives, chopped (for garnish)

Instructions:

Preheat Oven:
- Preheat your oven to 350°F (175°C). Grease a 9x13-inch baking dish.

Prepare Eggs Mixture:
- In a large bowl, whisk together the eggs, milk, Dijon mustard, salt, and pepper until well combined.

Assemble Casserole:
- Place the cubed bread in the prepared baking dish. Pour the egg mixture over the bread, ensuring it's evenly distributed.

Add Cheese and Spinach:
- Sprinkle the shredded cheddar cheese over the bread and egg mixture. Add the chopped spinach (and any optional ingredients like diced ham, onions, or bell peppers) evenly.

Drizzle with Butter:
- Drizzle the melted butter over the top of the casserole.

Let it Sit:
- Allow the casserole to sit for about 10-15 minutes, giving the bread time to absorb the egg mixture.

Bake:
- Bake in the preheated oven for 35-40 minutes or until the top is golden brown, and the center is set.

Garnish:

- Remove the casserole from the oven and let it rest for a few minutes. Garnish with fresh parsley or chives.

Slice and Serve:

- Slice into squares or rectangles and serve warm.

Enjoy:

- Enjoy this hearty and flavorful Cheese and Spinach Breakfast Casserole for a delicious breakfast or brunch!

This Cheese and Spinach Breakfast Casserole is not only easy to make but also versatile. You can customize it with your favorite ingredients, and it's perfect for feeding a crowd. The combination of eggs, cheese, spinach, and bread makes for a satisfying and comforting breakfast option.

Cheese and Ham Quiche

Ingredients:

For the Pie Crust:

- 1 1/4 cups all-purpose flour
- 1/2 cup unsalted butter, cold and diced
- 1/4 teaspoon salt
- 3-4 tablespoons ice water

For the Quiche Filling:

- 1 cup cooked ham, diced
- 1 1/2 cups shredded Swiss cheese
- 1/2 cup shredded cheddar cheese
- 4 large eggs
- 1 cup whole milk
- 1/2 cup heavy cream
- 1/4 teaspoon salt
- 1/4 teaspoon black pepper
- 1/4 teaspoon ground nutmeg (optional)
- 2 tablespoons all-purpose flour (to coat ham)

Instructions:

For the Pie Crust:

Prepare Pie Crust:
- In a food processor, combine the flour, cold diced butter, and salt. Pulse until the mixture resembles coarse crumbs.

Add Ice Water:
- Gradually add ice water, one tablespoon at a time, and pulse until the dough just comes together.

Form Dough:
- Turn the dough out onto a floured surface, shape it into a disk, wrap in plastic wrap, and refrigerate for at least 30 minutes.

Roll Out Crust:
- Roll out the chilled dough on a floured surface to fit a 9-inch pie dish. Press the dough into the pie dish, trim any excess, and flute the edges.

Prebake Crust:
- Prebake the crust in a preheated oven at 375°F (190°C) for about 10 minutes or until it just starts to set. Remove from the oven and let it cool slightly.

For the Quiche Filling:

Preheat Oven:
- Preheat your oven to 375°F (190°C).

Coat Ham with Flour:
- In a small bowl, toss the diced ham with 2 tablespoons of flour. This helps to prevent the ham from sinking to the bottom of the quiche.

Assemble Quiche:
- Spread the coated ham evenly over the prebaked pie crust. Sprinkle the shredded Swiss cheese and cheddar cheese over the ham.

Whisk Egg Mixture:
- In a separate bowl, whisk together the eggs, whole milk, heavy cream, salt, black pepper, and nutmeg (if using).

Pour Over Cheese and Ham:
- Pour the egg mixture over the cheese and ham in the pie crust.

Bake:
- Bake in the preheated oven for 35-40 minutes or until the quiche is set and the top is golden brown.

Cool:
- Allow the quiche to cool for a few minutes before slicing.

Slice and Serve:
- Slice into wedges and serve warm.

Enjoy:
- Enjoy this savory and comforting Cheese and Ham Quiche for breakfast, brunch, or any meal!

Feel free to customize the quiche by adding vegetables like sautéed mushrooms or spinach. This versatile recipe is great for using up leftover ham and creating a satisfying and flavorful dish.

Cheese Danish

Ingredients:

For the Dough:

- 2 1/4 teaspoons (1 packet) active dry yeast
- 1/4 cup warm water (about 110°F or 43°C)
- 1/2 cup milk, room temperature
- 1/4 cup granulated sugar
- 1/2 cup unsalted butter, softened
- 1/2 teaspoon salt
- 2 large eggs
- 2 1/2 cups all-purpose flour, plus more for dusting

For the Cheese Filling:

- 8 ounces cream cheese, softened
- 1/4 cup granulated sugar
- 1 teaspoon vanilla extract
- 1 tablespoon lemon juice (optional)

For the Glaze:

- 1 cup powdered sugar
- 2 tablespoons milk
- 1/2 teaspoon vanilla extract

Instructions:

For the Dough:

Activate Yeast:
- In a small bowl, dissolve the yeast in warm water. Let it sit for about 5 minutes until it becomes frothy.

Prepare Dough:
- In a large mixing bowl, combine the activated yeast, milk, sugar, softened butter, salt, eggs, and 2 1/2 cups of flour. Mix until the dough comes together.

Knead Dough:

- Turn the dough onto a floured surface and knead for about 5-7 minutes or until it becomes smooth and elastic. Add more flour as needed to prevent sticking.

First Rise:
- Place the dough in a greased bowl, cover with a clean kitchen towel, and let it rise in a warm place for about 1-1.5 hours or until doubled in size.

For the Cheese Filling:

Prepare Cheese Filling:
- In a bowl, combine the softened cream cheese, sugar, vanilla extract, and lemon juice (if using). Mix until smooth and well combined.

Assembling the Cheese Danish:

Preheat Oven:
- Preheat your oven to 375°F (190°C) and line a baking sheet with parchment paper.

Roll Out Dough:
- Roll out the risen dough on a floured surface into a rectangle, about 16x12 inches.

Spread Cheese Filling:
- Spread the prepared cheese filling evenly over the rolled-out dough.

Shape Danish:
- Fold the dough in half lengthwise to cover the filling, creating a long rectangle. Cut the dough into strips, and then cut each strip diagonally to form triangles.

Shape into Crescents:
- Roll each triangle from the wide end to the point, shaping it into a crescent.

Second Rise:
- Place the shaped Danish on the prepared baking sheet and let them rise for an additional 15-20 minutes.

Bake:
- Bake in the preheated oven for 12-15 minutes or until the Danish are golden brown.

For the Glaze:

Prepare Glaze:

- In a bowl, whisk together powdered sugar, milk, and vanilla extract until smooth.

Glaze Danish:

- Drizzle the glaze over the warm Danish immediately after removing them from the oven.

Cool:

- Allow the Cheese Danish to cool slightly before serving.

Enjoy:

- Enjoy these homemade Cheese Danish for breakfast or as a delightful sweet treat!

These Cheese Danish are soft, flaky, and filled with a creamy cheese filling. The sweet glaze adds the perfect finishing touch. They are perfect for a special breakfast or brunch.

Cheese and Tomato Breakfast Sandwich

Ingredients:

- 1 English muffin, split and toasted
- 1 large egg
- Salt and pepper, to taste
- 1 slice of your favorite cheese (cheddar, Swiss, or mozzarella work well)
- 1 medium-sized tomato, sliced
- Fresh basil leaves (optional, for added flavor)

Instructions:

Prepare English Muffin:
- Split the English muffin and toast it to your liking.

Cook the Egg:
- In a small skillet, cook the egg to your preference (fried, scrambled, or poached). Season with salt and pepper to taste.

Add Cheese:
- Place the slice of cheese on top of the cooked egg in the skillet. Allow it to melt slightly.

Assemble Sandwich:
- Place the cheesy egg on the bottom half of the toasted English muffin.

Add Tomato Slices:
- Arrange tomato slices on top of the cheesy egg. Add fresh basil leaves if desired.

Top with Second Half:
- Place the other half of the toasted English muffin on top to create the sandwich.

Serve:
- Serve the Cheese and Tomato Breakfast Sandwich immediately while it's warm and the cheese is melted.

Enjoy:
- Enjoy this quick and tasty breakfast sandwich with the combination of gooey cheese, juicy tomatoes, and a perfectly cooked egg!

Feel free to customize this sandwich by adding other ingredients like avocado, bacon, or spinach to suit your taste preferences. It's a versatile and satisfying breakfast option.

Breads and Rolls:

Garlic Parmesan Breadsticks

Ingredients:

For the Breadsticks:

- 1 pound pizza dough (store-bought or homemade)
- 2 tablespoons unsalted butter, melted
- 2 cloves garlic, minced
- 1/4 cup grated Parmesan cheese
- 1/2 teaspoon dried oregano
- 1/2 teaspoon dried parsley
- Salt, to taste

For the Dipping Sauce:

- 1/2 cup marinara sauce (store-bought or homemade)

Instructions:

For the Breadsticks:

Preheat Oven:
- Preheat your oven to 400°F (200°C). Line a baking sheet with parchment paper.

Prepare Dough:
- If using store-bought pizza dough, let it come to room temperature. If making homemade dough, follow your recipe.

Roll Out Dough:
- On a lightly floured surface, roll out the pizza dough into a rectangle, about 12x8 inches.

Brush with Garlic Butter:
- In a small bowl, mix the melted butter and minced garlic. Brush the entire surface of the rolled-out dough with the garlic butter mixture.

Sprinkle Parmesan and Herbs:
- Sprinkle the grated Parmesan cheese, dried oregano, dried parsley, and a pinch of salt evenly over the garlic buttered dough.

Cut into Strips:

- Using a pizza cutter or a sharp knife, cut the dough into strips, about 1 inch wide.

Twist the Strips:
- Twist each strip and place it on the prepared baking sheet. Press the ends onto the sheet to secure.

Bake:
- Bake in the preheated oven for 12-15 minutes or until the breadsticks are golden brown.

Optional: Additional Topping:
- Optionally, when the breadsticks are hot out of the oven, brush them with a little more garlic butter and sprinkle additional Parmesan cheese if desired.

For the Dipping Sauce:

Warm Marinara Sauce:
- While the breadsticks are baking, warm the marinara sauce in a small saucepan or in the microwave.

Serve:
- Serve the Garlic Parmesan Breadsticks warm with the marinara sauce for dipping.

Enjoy:
- Enjoy these homemade breadsticks as a tasty appetizer or side dish!

These Garlic Parmesan Breadsticks are flavorful, soft on the inside, and have a deliciously crispy exterior. The combination of garlic, Parmesan, and herbs makes them a delightful addition to any meal or a perfect snack.

Cheddar Jalapeños Cornbread

Ingredients:

- 1 cup yellow cornmeal
- 1 cup all-purpose flour
- 1 tablespoon baking powder
- 1/2 teaspoon baking soda
- 1/2 teaspoon salt
- 1 cup buttermilk
- 2 large eggs
- 1/4 cup unsalted butter, melted
- 1 cup shredded sharp cheddar cheese
- 1/4 cup pickled jalapeños, chopped (adjust to taste)
- 1/4 cup fresh cilantro, chopped (optional, for garnish)

Instructions:

Preheat Oven:
- Preheat your oven to 400°F (200°C). Grease a square or round baking pan.

Mix Dry Ingredients:
- In a large bowl, whisk together the cornmeal, flour, baking powder, baking soda, and salt.

Combine Wet Ingredients:
- In another bowl, whisk together the buttermilk, eggs, and melted butter.

Combine Wet and Dry Ingredients:
- Pour the wet ingredients into the dry ingredients and stir until just combined. Be careful not to overmix.

Add Cheese and Jalapeños:
- Gently fold in the shredded cheddar cheese and chopped jalapeños into the batter.

Transfer to Baking Pan:
- Pour the batter into the prepared baking pan, spreading it evenly.

Bake:
- Bake in the preheated oven for about 20-25 minutes or until the top is golden brown and a toothpick inserted into the center comes out clean.

Cool:
- Allow the cornbread to cool in the pan for a few minutes, then transfer it to a wire rack to cool completely.

Garnish (Optional):

- If desired, garnish with chopped fresh cilantro.

Slice and Serve:

- Once cooled, slice the cornbread into squares or wedges. Serve it warm.

Enjoy:

- Enjoy the Cheddar Jalapeño Cornbread as a delicious side dish to complement soups, stews, or as a standalone treat!

This cornbread has a perfect balance of savory cheddar and a hint of heat from the jalapeños, making it a flavorful and slightly spicy twist on traditional cornbread. Adjust the amount of jalapeños based on your spice preference.

Cheese and Herb Focaccia

Ingredients:

For the Focaccia Dough:

- 1 3/4 cups warm water (about 110°F or 43°C)
- 1 tablespoon sugar
- 2 1/4 teaspoons (1 packet) active dry yeast
- 4 1/4 cups all-purpose flour
- 2 teaspoons salt
- 1/2 cup olive oil (divided)

For Topping:

- 1 cup shredded mozzarella cheese
- 1/2 cup grated Parmesan cheese
- 2 tablespoons fresh rosemary, chopped
- 2 tablespoons fresh thyme, chopped
- Coarse sea salt, for sprinkling

Instructions:

Prepare the Focaccia Dough:

Activate Yeast:
- In a bowl, combine warm water, sugar, and active dry yeast. Let it sit for about 5-10 minutes until the yeast is foamy.

Mix Dry Ingredients:
- In a large mixing bowl, combine flour and salt.

Combine Wet and Dry Ingredients:
- Make a well in the center of the flour mixture. Pour in the activated yeast mixture and 1/4 cup of olive oil. Mix until a dough forms.

Knead Dough:
- Turn the dough onto a floured surface and knead for about 8-10 minutes until it becomes smooth and elastic.

First Rise:
- Place the dough in a lightly oiled bowl, cover it with a clean kitchen towel, and let it rise in a warm place for about 1-1.5 hours or until doubled in size.

Assemble the Focaccia:

Preheat Oven:
- Preheat your oven to 425°F (220°C). Grease a baking sheet or line it with parchment paper.

Stretch Dough:
- Transfer the risen dough to the prepared baking sheet. Gently stretch and press the dough to cover the entire surface of the baking sheet.

Create Indents:
- Use your fingertips to create dimples or indents all over the surface of the dough.

Drizzle with Olive Oil:
- Drizzle the remaining 1/4 cup of olive oil over the surface of the dough.

Add Toppings:
- Sprinkle shredded mozzarella, grated Parmesan, fresh rosemary, and fresh thyme evenly over the dough. Press the toppings slightly into the dough.

Sprinkle with Sea Salt:
- Sprinkle coarse sea salt over the top for added flavor.

Second Rise:
- Allow the assembled focaccia to rise for an additional 20-30 minutes.

Bake:
- Bake in the preheated oven for 20-25 minutes or until the focaccia is golden brown and cooked through.

Cool:
- Allow the focaccia to cool slightly before slicing.

Slice and Serve:
- Slice the Cheese and Herb Focaccia into squares or rectangles. Serve warm.

Enjoy:
- Enjoy this flavorful Cheese and Herb Focaccia as a delightful appetizer or side dish!

This Cheese and Herb Focaccia is soft on the inside with a crispy exterior, and the combination of cheeses and fresh herbs makes it a delightful treat. It's perfect for sharing at gatherings or enjoying with your favorite dips.

Swiss Cheese and Onion Bread

Ingredients:

For the Dough:

- 3 cups all-purpose flour
- 1 tablespoon sugar
- 1 tablespoon active dry yeast
- 1 cup warm milk (about 110°F or 43°C)
- 1/4 cup unsalted butter, melted
- 1 teaspoon salt

For the Filling:

- 1 large onion, finely chopped
- 2 tablespoons unsalted butter
- 1 1/2 cups shredded Swiss cheese
- 1 teaspoon dried thyme (optional)
- Salt and black pepper, to taste

For Topping:

- 1/2 cup shredded Swiss cheese

Instructions:

Prepare the Dough:

Activate Yeast:
- In a bowl, combine warm milk, sugar, and active dry yeast. Let it sit for about 5-10 minutes until the yeast is foamy.

Mix Dry Ingredients:
- In a large mixing bowl, combine flour and salt.

Combine Wet and Dry Ingredients:
- Make a well in the center of the flour mixture. Pour in the activated yeast mixture and melted butter. Mix until a dough forms.

Knead Dough:
- Turn the dough onto a floured surface and knead for about 8-10 minutes until it becomes smooth and elastic.

First Rise:

- Place the dough in a lightly oiled bowl, cover it with a clean kitchen towel, and let it rise in a warm place for about 1-1.5 hours or until doubled in size.

Prepare the Filling:

Sauté Onions:
- In a skillet, melt 2 tablespoons of butter over medium heat. Add the finely chopped onions and sauté until soft and golden brown. Season with salt and black pepper. Set aside to cool.

Roll Out Dough:
- Roll out the risen dough on a floured surface into a rectangle.

Spread Filling:
- Spread the sautéed onions evenly over the dough. Sprinkle shredded Swiss cheese and dried thyme (if using) over the onions.

Roll the Dough:
- Roll the dough from one of the longer sides to form a log. Pinch the seam to seal.

Slice into Portions:
- Using a sharp knife, slice the rolled dough into portions, about 1-1.5 inches wide.

Arrange in Pan:
- Place the sliced portions in a greased baking dish, leaving some space between each piece.

Second Rise:
- Allow the arranged dough to rise for an additional 20-30 minutes.

Preheat Oven:
- Preheat your oven to 375°F (190°C).

Top with Cheese:
- Sprinkle the remaining 1/2 cup of shredded Swiss cheese over the top of the dough.

Bake:
- Bake in the preheated oven for 25-30 minutes or until the bread is golden brown and cooked through.

Cool:
- Allow the Swiss Cheese and Onion Bread to cool slightly before serving.

Enjoy:
- Enjoy this flavorful bread as a savory side or snack!

This Swiss Cheese and Onion Bread is a delightful combination of soft, fluffy bread, savory sautéed onions, and gooey Swiss cheese. It's perfect for sharing and adds a delicious twist to your bread repertoire.

Cheese-Stuffed Pretzels

Ingredients:

For the Pretzel Dough:

- 1 1/2 cups warm water (about 110°F or 43°C)
- 1 tablespoon granulated sugar
- 2 teaspoons active dry yeast
- 4 1/2 cups all-purpose flour
- 1 teaspoon salt
- 2 tablespoons unsalted butter, melted

For the Cheese Filling:

- 2 cups shredded cheddar cheese
- 1 cup mozzarella cheese, shredded
- 1 teaspoon garlic powder
- 1/2 teaspoon onion powder
- Salt and black pepper, to taste

For Boiling and Topping:

- 10 cups water
- 2/3 cup baking soda
- 1 large egg, beaten (for egg wash)
- Coarse salt, for sprinkling

Instructions:

Prepare the Pretzel Dough:

Activate Yeast:
- In a bowl, combine warm water, sugar, and active dry yeast. Let it sit for about 5-10 minutes until the yeast is foamy.

Mix Dough:
- In a large mixing bowl, combine the flour, salt, melted butter, and the activated yeast mixture. Mix until a dough forms.

Knead Dough:
- Turn the dough onto a floured surface and knead for about 8-10 minutes until it becomes smooth and elastic.

First Rise:
- Place the dough in a lightly oiled bowl, cover it with a clean kitchen towel, and let it rise in a warm place for about 1-1.5 hours or until doubled in size.

Prepare the Cheese Filling:

Mix Cheeses and Seasonings:
- In a bowl, combine shredded cheddar cheese, mozzarella cheese, garlic powder, onion powder, salt, and black pepper. Mix well.

Divide into Portions:
- Divide the cheese mixture into portions to be used for stuffing each pretzel.

Assemble the Cheese-Stuffed Pretzels:

Preheat Oven:
- Preheat your oven to 450°F (230°C). Line a baking sheet with parchment paper.

Divide Dough:
- Punch down the risen dough and divide it into equal portions, depending on the number of pretzels you want.

Roll Out Dough:
- Roll each portion into a rope, about 24 inches long.

Stuff with Cheese:
- Flatten each rope and place a portion of the cheese filling in the center. Fold the dough over the cheese and pinch the edges to seal.

Shape into Pretzels:
- Twist each filled rope into a pretzel shape and place it on the prepared baking sheet.

Boil Pretzels:
- In a large pot, bring 10 cups of water to a boil. Add baking soda. Boil each pretzel for about 30 seconds to 1 minute, then remove and place back on the baking sheet.

Brush with Egg Wash:
- Brush each pretzel with beaten egg and sprinkle coarse salt over the top.

Bake:
- Bake in the preheated oven for 12-15 minutes or until the pretzels are golden brown.

Cool:

- Allow the Cheese-Stuffed Pretzels to cool slightly before serving.

Enjoy:
- Enjoy these warm, gooey Cheese-Stuffed Pretzels as a delightful snack or appetizer!

These Cheese-Stuffed Pretzels are a perfect combination of soft pretzel dough and gooey melted cheese. They make a delicious and satisfying treat for any occasion.

Printed in the USA
CPSIA information can be obtained
at www.ICGtesting.com
LVHW080935160424
777536LV00010B/365

9 798869 186959